Book Log

Ruth DuCharme

ISBN:1725946246
ISBN-13:9781725946248

Date Read_____________

Book Title ____

Author____

I give this book _________ stars ★ ★ ★ ★ ★

What I enjoyed about the book

____

____

____

____

____

____

____

What I didn't enjoy about this book

____

____

____

____

____

____

____

What I will do with this book now?

- o   Donate
- o   Gift it
- o   Save it so I can read it again

Date Read_______________

Book Title ____

Author____

I give this book _________ stars ★★★★★

What I enjoyed about the book

____
____
____
____
____
____
____
____

What I didn't enjoy about this book

____
____
____
____
____
____
____
____

What I will do with this book now?

- ○ Donate
- ○ Gift it
- ○ Save it so I can read it again

Date Read_____________

Book Title ____

Author____

I give this book _________ stars ★ ★ ★ ★ ★

What I enjoyed about the book

____
____
____
____
____
____
____
____

What I didn't enjoy about this book

____
____
____
____
____
____
____
____
____

What I will do with this book now?

- ○ Donate
- ○ Gift it
- ○ Save it so I can read it again

Date Read______________

Book Title ____

Author____

I give this book _________ stars ★★★★★

What I enjoyed about the book

____
____
____
____
____
____
____
____

What I didn't enjoy about this book

____
____
____
____
____
____
____
____

What I will do with this book now?

- o Donate
- o Gift it
- o Save it so I can read it again

Date Read_____________

Book Title ____

Author____

I give this book _________ stars ★ ★ ★ ★ ★

What I enjoyed about the book

____
____
____
____
____
____
____
____

What I didn't enjoy about this book

____
____
____
____
____
____
____
____

What I will do with this book now?

- o   Donate
- o   Gift it
- o   Save it so I can read it again

My Book Log

Date Read_____________

Book Title ____

Author____

I give this book _________ stars   ★ ★ ★ ★ ★

What I enjoyed about the book

____
____
____
____
____
____
____
____

What I didn't enjoy about this book

____
____
____
____
____
____
____
____

What I will do with this book now?

- o   Donate
- o   Gift it
- o   Save it so I can read it again

Date Read____________

Book Title ____

Author____

I give this book _________ stars ★ ★ ★ ★ ★

What I enjoyed about the book

____
____
____
____
____
____
____
____

What I didn't enjoy about this book

____
____
____
____
____
____
____
____

What I will do with this book now?

- o Donate
- o Gift it
- o Save it so I can read it again

My Book Log

Date Read____________

Book Title ____

Author____

I give this book ________ stars ★★★★★

What I enjoyed about the book

____
____
____
____
____
____
____
____

What I didn't enjoy about this book

____
____
____
____
____
____
____
____

What I will do with this book now?

- Donate
- Gift it
- Save it so I can read it again

My Book Log

Date Read_____________

Book Title ____

Author____

I give this book _________ stars

What I enjoyed about the book

____

____

____

____

____

____

____

____

What I didn't enjoy about this book

____

____

____

____

____

____

____

____

What I will do with this book now?

- o   Donate
- o   Gift it
- o   Save it so I can read it again

My Book Log

Date Read_______________

Book Title ____

Author____

I give this book _________ stars ★ ★ ★ ★ ★

What I enjoyed about the book

____
____
____
____
____
____
____
____

What I didn't enjoy about this book

____
____
____
____
____
____
____

What I will do with this book now?

- o   Donate
- o   Gift it
- o   Save it so I can read it again

Date Read____________

Book Title ____

Author____

I give this book _________ stars ★ ★ ★ ★ ★

What I enjoyed about the book

____

____

____

____

____

____

____

____

What I didn't enjoy about this book

____

____

____

____

____

____

____

____

What I will do with this book now?

- o Donate
- o Gift it
- o Save it so I can read it again

Date Read_____________

Book Title ____

Author____

I give this book _________ stars

What I enjoyed about the book

____
____
____
____
____
____
____
____

What I didn't enjoy about this book

____
____
____
____
____
____
____
____

What I will do with this book now?

- o Donate
- o Gift it
- o Save it so I can read it again

Date Read____________

Book Title ____

Author____

I give this book _________ stars ★ ★ ★ ★ ★

What I enjoyed about the book

____
____
____
____
____
____
____

What I didn't enjoy about this book

____
____
____
____
____
____
____

What I will do with this book now?

- Donate
- Gift it
- Save it so I can read it again

Date Read____________

Book Title ____

Author____

I give this book _________ stars

What I enjoyed about the book

____
____
____
____
____
____
____
____

What I didn't enjoy about this book

____
____
____
____
____
____
____
____

What I will do with this book now?

- ○ Donate
- ○ Gift it
- ○ Save it so I can read it again

Date Read_____________

Book Title ____

Author____

I give this book _________ stars ★ ★ ★ ★ ★

What I enjoyed about the book

____
____
____
____
____
____
____
____

What I didn't enjoy about this book

____
____
____
____
____
____
____
____

What I will do with this book now?

- o Donate
- o Gift it
- o Save it so I can read it again

Date Read______________

Book Title ____

Author____

I give this book _________ stars ★★★★★

What I enjoyed about the book

____
____
____
____
____
____
____
____

What I didn't enjoy about this book

____
____
____
____
____
____
____

What I will do with this book now?

- o   Donate
- o   Gift it
- o   Save it so I can read it again

Date Read____________

Book Title ____

Author____

I give this book _________ stars ★ ★ ★ ★ ★

What I enjoyed about the book

____

____

____

____

____

____

____

____

What I didn't enjoy about this book

____

____

____

____

____

____

____

What I will do with this book now?

- o   Donate
- o   Gift it
- o   Save it so I can read it again

My Book Log

Date Read_____________

Book Title ____

Author____

I give this book _________ stars ★ ★ ★ ★ ★

What I enjoyed about the book

____
____
____
____
____
____
____
____

What I didn't enjoy about this book

____
____
____
____
____
____
____

What I will do with this book now?

- o   Donate
- o   Gift it
- o   Save it so I can read it again

Date Read_____________

Book Title ____

Author____

I give this book _________ stars ★ ★ ★ ★ ★

What I enjoyed about the book

____
____
____
____
____
____
____
____

What I didn't enjoy about this book

____
____
____
____
____
____
____

What I will do with this book now?

- o   Donate
- o   Gift it
- o   Save it so I can read it again

Date Read_____________

Book Title ____

Author____

I give this book _________ stars ★ ★ ★ ★ ★

What I enjoyed about the book

____

____

____

____

____

____

____

What I didn't enjoy about this book

____

____

____

____

____

____

____

What I will do with this book now?

- o Donate
- o Gift it
- o Save it so I can read it again

Date Read____________

Book Title ____

Author____

I give this book ________ stars   ★ ★ ★ ★ ★

What I enjoyed about the book

____

____

____

____

____

____

____

What I didn't enjoy about this book

____

____

____

____

____

____

____

What I will do with this book now?

- o   Donate
- o   Gift it
- o   Save it so I can read it again

My Book Log

Date Read_____________

Book Title ____

Author____

I give this book _________ stars ★ ★ ★ ★ ★

What I enjoyed about the book

____

____

____

____

____

____

____

____

What I didn't enjoy about this book

____

____

____

____

____

____

____

____

What I will do with this book now?

- o   Donate
- o   Gift it
- o   Save it so I can read it again

Date Read______________

Book Title ____

Author____

I give this book __________ stars ★ ★ ★ ★ ★

What I enjoyed about the book

____

____

____

____

____

____

____

What I didn't enjoy about this book

____

____

____

____

____

____

____

What I will do with this book now?

- o   Donate
- o   Gift it
- o   Save it so I can read it again

My Book Log

Date Read______________

Book Title ____

Author____

I give this book _________ stars ★ ★ ★ ★ ★

What I enjoyed about the book

____
____
____
____
____
____
____
____

What I didn't enjoy about this book

____
____
____
____
____
____
____
____

What I will do with this book now?

- o   Donate
- o   Gift it
- o   Save it so I can read it again

My Book Log

Date Read____________

Book Title ____

Author____

I give this book _________ stars   ★ ★ ★ ★ ★

What I enjoyed about the book

____
____
____
____
____
____
____
____

What I didn't enjoy about this book

____
____
____
____
____
____
____
____

What I will do with this book now?

- o   Donate
- o   Gift it
- o   Save it so I can read it again

My Book Log

Date Read______________

Book Title ____

Author____

I give this book __________ stars ★ ★ ★ ★ ★

What I enjoyed about the book

____

____

____

____

____

____

____

____

What I didn't enjoy about this book

____

____

____

____

____

____

____

____

What I will do with this book now?

- o   Donate
- o   Gift it
- o   Save it so I can read it again

Date Read_____________

Book Title ____

Author____

I give this book _________ stars ★ ★ ★ ★ ★

What I enjoyed about the book

____
____
____
____
____
____
____
____

What I didn't enjoy about this book

____
____
____
____
____
____
____
____

What I will do with this book now?

- o Donate
- o Gift it
- o Save it so I can read it again

Date Read_____________

Book Title ____

Author____

I give this book _________ stars

What I enjoyed about the book

____

____

____

____

____

____

____

____

What I didn't enjoy about this book

____

____

____

____

____

____

____

What I will do with this book now?

- o   Donate
- o   Gift it
- o   Save it so I can read it again

Date Read____________

Book Title ____

Author____

I give this book _________ stars ★ ★ ★ ★ ★

What I enjoyed about the book

____
____
____
____
____
____
____

What I didn't enjoy about this book

____
____
____
____
____
____
____

What I will do with this book now?

- o   Donate
- o   Gift it
- o   Save it so I can read it again

Date Read_____________

Book Title ____

Author____

I give this book _________ stars ★ ★ ★ ★ ★

What I enjoyed about the book

____
____
____
____
____
____
____
____

What I didn't enjoy about this book

____
____
____
____
____
____
____
____

What I will do with this book now?

- Donate
- Gift it
- Save it so I can read it again

Date Read____________

Book Title ____

Author____

I give this book _________ stars ★ ★ ★ ★ ★

What I enjoyed about the book

____
____
____
____
____
____
____
____

What I didn't enjoy about this book

____
____
____
____
____
____
____
____

What I will do with this book now?

- o   Donate
- o   Gift it
- o   Save it so I can read it again

Date Read_______________

Book Title ____

Author____

I give this book _________ stars ★ ★ ★ ★ ★

What I enjoyed about the book

____
____
____
____
____
____
____
____

What I didn't enjoy about this book

____
____
____
____
____
____
____
____

What I will do with this book now?

- Donate
- Gift it
- Save it so I can read it again

Date Read____________

Book Title ____

Author____

I give this book _________ stars ★ ★ ★ ★ ★

What I enjoyed about the book

____

____

____

____

____

____

____

What I didn't enjoy about this book

____

____

____

____

____

____

____

What I will do with this book now?

- o   Donate
- o   Gift it
- o   Save it so I can read it again

Date Read____________

Book Title ____

Author____

I give this book _________ stars ★ ★ ★ ★ ★

What I enjoyed about the book

____
____
____
____
____
____
____
____

What I didn't enjoy about this book

____
____
____
____
____
____
____

What I will do with this book now?

- o   Donate
- o   Gift it
- o   Save it so I can read it again

Date Read____________

Book Title ____

Author____

I give this book _________ stars ★ ★ ★ ★ ★

What I enjoyed about the book

____
____
____
____
____
____
____
____

What I didn't enjoy about this book

____
____
____
____
____
____
____
____

What I will do with this book now?

- o   Donate
- o   Gift it
- o   Save it so I can read it again

Date Read____________

Book Title ____

Author____

I give this book ________ stars ★ ★ ★ ★ ★

What I enjoyed about the book

____

____

____

____

____

____

____

____

What I didn't enjoy about this book

____

____

____

____

____

____

____

What I will do with this book now?

- ○ Donate
- ○ Gift it
- ○ Save it so I can read it again

Date Read______________

Book Title ____

Author____

I give this book _________ stars ★ ★ ★ ★ ★

What I enjoyed about the book

____
____
____
____
____
____
____
____

What I didn't enjoy about this book

____
____
____
____
____
____
____
____

What I will do with this book now?

- o   Donate
- o   Gift it
- o   Save it so I can read it again

Date Read______________

Book Title ____

Author____

I give this book _________ stars ★ ★ ★ ★ ★

What I enjoyed about the book

____

____

____

____

____

____

____

____

What I didn't enjoy about this book

____

____

____

____

____

____

____

____

What I will do with this book now?

- Donate
- Gift it
- Save it so I can read it again

Date Read______________

Book Title ____

Author____

I give this book _________ stars   ★ ★ ★ ★ ★

What I enjoyed about the book

____
____
____
____
____
____
____

What I didn't enjoy about this book

____
____
____
____
____
____
____

What I will do with this book now?

- o   Donate
- o   Gift it
- o   Save it so I can read it again

Date Read____________

Book Title ____

Author____

I give this book _________ stars ★ ★ ★ ★ ★

What I enjoyed about the book

____

____

____

____

____

____

____

____

What I didn't enjoy about this book

____

____

____

____

____

____

____

____

What I will do with this book now?

- o   Donate
- o   Gift it
- o   Save it so I can read it again

Date Read_____________

Book Title ____

Author____

I give this book _________ stars ★ ★ ★ ★ ★

What I enjoyed about the book

____
____
____
____
____
____
____
____

What I didn't enjoy about this book

____
____
____
____
____
____
____
____

What I will do with this book now?

- o   Donate
- o   Gift it
- o   Save it so I can read it again

My Book Log

Date Read_____________

Book Title ____

Author____

I give this book ________ stars ★ ★ ★ ★ ★

What I enjoyed about the book

____
____
____
____
____
____
____
____

What I didn't enjoy about this book

____
____
____
____
____
____
____
____

What I will do with this book now?

- o   Donate
- o   Gift it
- o   Save it so I can read it again

Date Read_____________

Book Title ____

Author____

I give this book _________ stars ★ ★ ★ ★ ★

What I enjoyed about the book

____
____
____
____
____
____
____
____

What I didn't enjoy about this book

____
____
____
____
____
____
____

What I will do with this book now?

- Donate
- Gift it
- Save it so I can read it again

Date Read_____________

Book Title ____

Author____

I give this book ________ stars   ★ ★ ★ ★ ★

What I enjoyed about the book

____
____
____
____
____
____
____
____

What I didn't enjoy about this book

____
____
____
____
____
____
____

What I will do with this book now?

- ○ Donate
- ○ Gift it
- ○ Save it so I can read it again

Date Read____________

Book Title ____

Author____

I give this book _________ stars ★ ★ ★ ★ ★

What I enjoyed about the book

____

____

____

____

____

____

____

____

What I didn't enjoy about this book

____

____

____

____

____

____

____

____

What I will do with this book now?

- o   Donate
- o   Gift it
- o   Save it so I can read it again

My Book Log

Date Read______________

Book Title ____

Author____

I give this book __________ stars ★ ★ ★ ★ ★

What I enjoyed about the book

____
____
____
____
____
____
____
____

What I didn't enjoy about this book

____
____
____
____
____
____
____
____

What I will do with this book now?

- o Donate
- o Gift it
- o Save it so I can read it again

My Book Log

Date Read____________

Book Title ____

Author____

I give this book _________ stars ★ ★ ★ ★ ★

What I enjoyed about the book

____
____
____
____
____
____
____
____

What I didn't enjoy about this book

____
____
____
____
____
____
____
____

What I will do with this book now?

- o Donate
- o Gift it
- o Save it so I can read it again

Date Read_______________

Book Title ____

Author____

I give this book _________ stars ★ ★ ★ ★ ★

What I enjoyed about the book

____
____
____
____
____
____
____
____

What I didn't enjoy about this book

____
____
____
____
____
____
____

What I will do with this book now?

- ○ Donate
- ○ Gift it
- ○ Save it so I can read it again

My Book Log

Date Read_____________

Book Title ____

Author____

I give this book _________ stars ★ ★ ★ ★ ★

What I enjoyed about the book

____
____
____
____
____
____
____
____

What I didn't enjoy about this book

____
____
____
____
____
____
____

What I will do with this book now?

- ○ Donate
- ○ Gift it
- ○ Save it so I can read it again

Date Read_______________

Book Title ____

Author____

I give this book _________ stars ★ ★ ★ ★ ★

What I enjoyed about the book

____

____

____

____

____

____

____

____

What I didn't enjoy about this book

____

____

____

____

____

____

____

____

What I will do with this book now?

- o   Donate
- o   Gift it
- o   Save it so I can read it again

Date Read_____________

Book Title ____

Author____

I give this book _________ stars ★ ★ ★ ★ ★

What I enjoyed about the book

____
____
____
____
____
____
____

What I didn't enjoy about this book

____
____
____
____
____
____
____

What I will do with this book now?

- o Donate
- o Gift it
- o Save it so I can read it again

Date Read_______________

Book Title ____

Author____

I give this book __________ stars ★ ★ ★ ★ ★

What I enjoyed about the book

____

____

____

____

____

____

____

____

What I didn't enjoy about this book

____

____

____

____

____

____

____

____

What I will do with this book now?

- o   Donate
- o   Gift it
- o   Save it so I can read it again

Date Read____________

Book Title ____

Author____

I give this book _________ stars ★ ★ ★ ★ ★

What I enjoyed about the book

____

____

____

____

____

____

____

____

What I didn't enjoy about this book

____

____

____

____

____

____

____

What I will do with this book now?

- o   Donate
- o   Gift it
- o   Save it so I can read it again

Date Read_______________

Book Title ____

Author____

I give this book _________ stars ★ ★ ★ ★ ★

What I enjoyed about the book

____
____
____
____
____
____
____
____

What I didn't enjoy about this book

____
____
____
____
____
____
____

What I will do with this book now?

- o   Donate
- o   Gift it
- o   Save it so I can read it again

Date Read____________

Book Title ____

Author____

I give this book _________ stars ★ ★ ★ ★ ★

What I enjoyed about the book

____
____
____
____
____
____
____

What I didn't enjoy about this book

____
____
____
____
____
____
____
____

What I will do with this book now?

- o   Donate
- o   Gift it
- o   Save it so I can read it again

Date Read_____________

Book Title ____

Author____

I give this book __________ stars ★ ★ ★ ★ ★

What I enjoyed about the book

____
____
____
____
____
____
____
____

What I didn't enjoy about this book

____
____
____
____
____
____
____
____

What I will do with this book now?

- ○ Donate
- ○ Gift it
- ○ Save it so I can read it again

Date Read_____________

Book Title ____

Author____

I give this book _________ stars ★ ★ ★ ★ ★

What I enjoyed about the book

____
____
____
____
____
____
____

What I didn't enjoy about this book

____
____
____
____
____
____
____

What I will do with this book now?

- o Donate
- o Gift it
- o Save it so I can read it again

Date Read_____________

Book Title ____

Author____

I give this book _________ stars   ★ ★ ★ ★ ★

What I enjoyed about the book

____
____
____
____
____
____
____

What I didn't enjoy about this book

____
____
____
____
____
____
____

What I will do with this book now?

- o   Donate
- o   Gift it
- o   Save it so I can read it again

Date Read____________

Book Title ____

Author____

I give this book _________ stars ★ ★ ★ ★ ★

What I enjoyed about the book

____

____

____

____

____

____

____

____

What I didn't enjoy about this book

____

____

____

____

____

____

____

____

What I will do with this book now?

- o   Donate
- o   Gift it
- o   Save it so I can read it again

My Book Log

Date Read_____________

Book Title ____

Author____

I give this book _________ stars   ★ ★ ★ ★ ★

What I enjoyed about the book

____

____

____

____

____

____

____

____

What I didn't enjoy about this book

____

____

____

____

____

____

____

What I will do with this book now?

- o   Donate
- o   Gift it
- o   Save it so I can read it again

Date Read____________

Book Title ____

Author____

I give this book _________ stars   ★ ★ ★ ★ ★

What I enjoyed about the book

____
____
____
____
____
____
____
____

What I didn't enjoy about this book

____
____
____
____
____
____
____

What I will do with this book now?

- o   Donate
- o   Gift it
- o   Save it so I can read it again

Date Read______________

Book Title ____

Author____

I give this book __________ stars   ★ ★ ★ ★ ★

What I enjoyed about the book

____

____

____

____

____

____

____

What I didn't enjoy about this book

____

____

____

____

____

____

____

What I will do with this book now?

- ○ Donate
- ○ Gift it
- ○ Save it so I can read it again

Date Read_____________

Book Title ____

Author____

I give this book _________ stars ★ ★ ★ ★ ★

What I enjoyed about the book

____
____
____
____
____
____
____
____

What I didn't enjoy about this book

____
____
____
____
____
____
____
____

What I will do with this book now?

- o   Donate
- o   Gift it
- o   Save it so I can read it again

My Book Log

Date Read_____________

Book Title ____

Author____

I give this book _________ stars ★ ★ ★ ★ ★

What I enjoyed about the book

____
____
____
____
____
____
____
____

What I didn't enjoy about this book

____
____
____
____
____
____
____
____

What I will do with this book now?

- o   Donate
- o   Gift it
- o   Save it so I can read it again

Date Read____________

Book Title ____

Author____

I give this book _________ stars ★ ★ ★ ★ ★

What I enjoyed about the book

____

____

____

____

____

____

____

____

What I didn't enjoy about this book

____

____

____

____

____

____

____

What I will do with this book now?

- o   Donate
- o   Gift it
- o   Save it so I can read it again

Date Read______________

Book Title ____

Author____

I give this book _________ stars ★ ★ ★ ★ ★

What I enjoyed about the book

____
____
____
____
____
____
____
____

What I didn't enjoy about this book

____
____
____
____
____
____
____
____

What I will do with this book now?

- o   Donate
- o   Gift it
- o   Save it so I can read it again

My Book Log

Date Read_____________

Book Title ____

Author____

I give this book _________ stars ★ ★ ★ ★ ★

What I enjoyed about the book

____
____
____
____
____
____
____

What I didn't enjoy about this book

____
____
____
____
____
____
____

What I will do with this book now?

- o Donate
- o Gift it
- o Save it so I can read it again

Date Read____________

Book Title ____

Author____

I give this book ________ stars

What I enjoyed about the book

____

____

____

____

____

____

____

What I didn't enjoy about this book

____

____

____

____

____

____

____

What I will do with this book now?

- o   Donate
- o   Gift it
- o   Save it so I can read it again

Date Read____________

Book Title ____

Author____

I give this book _________ stars ★ ★ ★ ★ ★

What I enjoyed about the book

____
____
____
____
____
____
____
____

What I didn't enjoy about this book

____
____
____
____
____
____
____
____

What I will do with this book now?

- o Donate
- o Gift it
- o Save it so I can read it again

My Book Log

Date Read____________

Book Title ____

Author____

I give this book _________ stars   ★ ★ ★ ★ ★

What I enjoyed about the book

____
____
____
____
____
____
____
____

What I didn't enjoy about this book

____
____
____
____
____
____
____
____

What I will do with this book now?

- o Donate
- o Gift it
- o Save it so I can read it again

Date Read_______________

Book Title ____

Author____

I give this book _________ stars ★ ★ ★ ★ ★

What I enjoyed about the book

____

____

____

____

____

____

____

What I didn't enjoy about this book

____

____

____

____

____

____

____

What I will do with this book now?

- o   Donate
- o   Gift it
- o   Save it so I can read it again

Date Read_______________

Book Title ____

Author____

I give this book _________ stars ★ ★ ★ ★ ★

What I enjoyed about the book

____

____

____

____

____

____

____

____

What I didn't enjoy about this book

____

____

____

____

____

____

____

What I will do with this book now?

- o   Donate
- o   Gift it
- o   Save it so I can read it again

Date Read______________

Book Title ____

Author____

I give this book __________ stars ★ ★ ★ ★ ★

What I enjoyed about the book

____
____
____
____
____
____
____
____

What I didn't enjoy about this book

____
____
____
____
____
____
____

What I will do with this book now?

- o   Donate
- o   Gift it
- o   Save it so I can read it again

Date Read_____________

Book Title ____

Author____

I give this book __________ stars

What I enjoyed about the book

____

____

____

____

____

____

____

____

What I didn't enjoy about this book

____

____

____

____

____

____

____

____

What I will do with this book now?

- o   Donate
- o   Gift it
- o   Save it so I can read it again

Date Read_____________

Book Title ____

Author____

I give this book _________ stars ★ ★ ★ ★ ★

What I enjoyed about the book

____
____
____
____
____
____
____

What I didn't enjoy about this book

____
____
____
____
____
____
____

What I will do with this book now?

- o   Donate
- o   Gift it
- o   Save it so I can read it again

My Book Log

Date Read______________

Book Title ____

Author____

I give this book __________ stars ★ ★ ★ ★ ★

What I enjoyed about the book

____
____
____
____
____
____
____
____

What I didn't enjoy about this book

____
____
____
____
____
____
____
____

What I will do with this book now?

- ○ Donate
- ○ Gift it
- ○ Save it so I can read it again

Date Read_____________

Book Title ____

Author____

I give this book _________ stars ★ ★ ★ ★ ★

What I enjoyed about the book

____

____

____

____

____

____

____

____

What I didn't enjoy about this book

____

____

____

____

____

____

____

____

What I will do with this book now?

- o   Donate
- o   Gift it
- o   Save it so I can read it again

Date Read_______________

Book Title ____

Author____

I give this book _________ stars ★ ★ ★ ★ ★

What I enjoyed about the book

____
____
____
____
____
____
____
____

What I didn't enjoy about this book

____
____
____
____
____
____
____
____

What I will do with this book now?

- o   Donate
- o   Gift it
- o   Save it so I can read it again

My Book Log

Date Read______________

Book Title ____

Author____

I give this book _________ stars ★ ★ ★ ★ ★

What I enjoyed about the book

____
____
____
____
____
____
____
____

What I didn't enjoy about this book

____
____
____
____
____
____
____
____

What I will do with this book now?

- Donate
- Gift it
- Save it so I can read it again

Date Read_____________

Book Title ____

Author____

I give this book _________ stars ★ ★ ★ ★ ★

What I enjoyed about the book

____
____
____
____
____
____
____
____

What I didn't enjoy about this book

____
____
____
____
____
____
____
____

What I will do with this book now?

- o   Donate
- o   Gift it
- o   Save it so I can read it again

Date Read_______________

Book Title ____

Author____

I give this book _________ stars ★ ★ ★ ★ ★

What I enjoyed about the book

____
____
____
____
____
____
____
____

What I didn't enjoy about this book

____
____
____
____
____
____
____

What I will do with this book now?

- o Donate
- o Gift it
- o Save it so I can read it again

My Book Log

Date Read______________

Book Title ____

Author____

I give this book _________ stars ★ ★ ★ ★ ★

What I enjoyed about the book

____

____

____

____

____

____

____

____

What I didn't enjoy about this book

____

____

____

____

____

____

____

____

What I will do with this book now?

- o   Donate
- o   Gift it
- o   Save it so I can read it again

Date Read_____________

Book Title ____

Author____

I give this book __________ stars ★ ★ ★ ★ ★

What I enjoyed about the book

____

____

____

____

____

____

____

What I didn't enjoy about this book

____

____

____

____

____

____

____

What I will do with this book now?

- o   Donate
- o   Gift it
- o   Save it so I can read it again

My Book Log

Date Read______________

Book Title ____

Author____

I give this book _________ stars   ★ ★ ★ ★ ★

What I enjoyed about the book

____

____

____

____

____

____

____

____

What I didn't enjoy about this book

____

____

____

____

____

____

____

What I will do with this book now?

- o   Donate
- o   Gift it
- o   Save it so I can read it again

My Book Log

Date Read_______________

Book Title ____

Author____

I give this book __________ stars ★ ★ ★ ★ ★

What I enjoyed about the book

____
____
____
____
____
____
____
____

What I didn't enjoy about this book

____
____
____
____
____
____
____
____

What I will do with this book now?

- o   Donate
- o   Gift it
- o   Save it so I can read it again

Date Read______________

Book Title ____

Author____

I give this book __________ stars ★ ★ ★ ★ ★

What I enjoyed about the book

____
____
____
____
____
____
____
____

What I didn't enjoy about this book

____
____
____
____
____
____
____
____

What I will do with this book now?

- o   Donate
- o   Gift it
- o   Save it so I can read it again

Date Read_____________

Book Title ____

Author____

I give this book _________ stars ★ ★ ★ ★ ★

What I enjoyed about the book

____

____

____

____

____

____

____

____

What I didn't enjoy about this book

____

____

____

____

____

____

____

____

What I will do with this book now?

- o Donate
- o Gift it
- o Save it so I can read it again

Date Read_______________

Book Title ____

Author____

I give this book __________ stars ★ ★ ★ ★ ★

What I enjoyed about the book

____
____
____
____
____
____
____
____

What I didn't enjoy about this book

____
____
____
____
____
____
____
____

What I will do with this book now?

- o Donate
- o Gift it
- o Save it so I can read it again

Date Read_____________

Book Title ____

Author____

I give this book _________ stars ★ ★ ★ ★ ★

What I enjoyed about the book

____

____

____

____

____

____

____

What I didn't enjoy about this book

____

____

____

____

____

____

____

What I will do with this book now?

- o   Donate
- o   Gift it
- o   Save it so I can read it again

Date Read_______________

Book Title ____

Author____

I give this book _________ stars ★ ★ ★ ★ ★

What I enjoyed about the book

____
____
____
____
____
____
____
____

What I didn't enjoy about this book

____
____
____
____
____
____
____

What I will do with this book now?

- o Donate
- o Gift it
- o Save it so I can read it again

My Book Log

Date Read______________

Book Title ____

Author____

I give this book _________ stars ★ ★ ★ ★ ★

What I enjoyed about the book

____
____
____
____
____
____
____
____

What I didn't enjoy about this book

____
____
____
____
____
____
____
____

What I will do with this book now?

- ○ Donate
- ○ Gift it
- ○ Save it so I can read it again

Date Read_______________

Book Title ____

Author____

I give this book _________ stars   ★ ★ ★ ★ ★

What I enjoyed about the book

____
____
____
____
____
____
____
____

What I didn't enjoy about this book

____
____
____
____
____
____
____
____

What I will do with this book now?

- ○ Donate
- ○ Gift it
- ○ Save it so I can read it again

Date Read_____________

Book Title ____

Author____

I give this book _________ stars ★ ★ ★ ★ ★

What I enjoyed about the book

____
____
____
____
____
____
____

What I didn't enjoy about this book

____
____
____
____
____
____
____

What I will do with this book now?

- o Donate
- o Gift it
- o Save it so I can read it again

Date Read___________

Book Title ____

Author____

I give this book ________ stars ★ ★ ★ ★ ★

What I enjoyed about the book

____
____
____
____
____
____
____
____

What I didn't enjoy about this book

____
____
____
____
____
____
____
____

What I will do with this book now?

- o   Donate
- o   Gift it
- o   Save it so I can read it again

Date Read_____________

Book Title ____

Author____

I give this book _________ stars ★ ★ ★ ★ ★

What I enjoyed about the book

____

____

____

____

____

____

____

____

What I didn't enjoy about this book

____

____

____

____

____

____

____

____

What I will do with this book now?

- o Donate
- o Gift it
- o Save it so I can read it again

Date Read______________

Book Title ____

Author____

I give this book _________ stars ★ ★ ★ ★ ★

What I enjoyed about the book

____
____
____
____
____
____
____

What I didn't enjoy about this book

____
____
____
____
____
____
____

What I will do with this book now?

- o   Donate
- o   Gift it
- o   Save it so I can read it again

My Book Log

Date Read____________

Book Title ____

Author____

I give this book _________ stars   ★ ★ ★ ★ ★

What I enjoyed about the book

____
____
____
____
____
____
____

What I didn't enjoy about this book

____
____
____
____
____
____
____

What I will do with this book now?

- ○ Donate
- ○ Gift it
- ○ Save it so I can read it again

Date Read_____________

Book Title ____

Author____

I give this book _________ stars ★ ★ ★ ★ ★

What I enjoyed about the book

____
____
____
____
____
____
____
____

What I didn't enjoy about this book

____
____
____
____
____
____
____
____

What I will do with this book now?

- o   Donate
- o   Gift it
- o   Save it so I can read it again

Date Read_____________

Book Title ____

Author____

I give this book _________ stars ★★★★★

What I enjoyed about the book

____
____
____
____
____
____
____

What I didn't enjoy about this book

____
____
____
____
____
____
____

What I will do with this book now?

- o Donate
- o Gift it
- o Save it so I can read it again

Date Read____________

Book Title ____

Author____

I give this book _________ stars ★ ★ ★ ★ ★

What I enjoyed about the book

____
____
____
____
____
____
____
____

What I didn't enjoy about this book

____
____
____
____
____
____
____
____

What I will do with this book now?

- o   Donate
- o   Gift it
- o   Save it so I can read it again

Date Read___________

Book Title _______________________________________

Author____

I give this book _________ stars ★ ★ ★ ★ ★

What I enjoyed about the book

____

____

____

____

____

____

____

____

What I didn't enjoy about this book

____

____

____

____

____

____

____

____

What I will do with this book now?

- o Donate
- o Gift it
- o Save it so I can read it again

Date Read_____________

Book Title ____

Author____

I give this book _________ stars ★ ★ ★ ★ ★

What I enjoyed about the book

____
____
____
____
____
____
____

What I didn't enjoy about this book

____
____
____
____
____
____
____

What I will do with this book now?

- ○ Donate
- ○ Gift it
- ○ Save it so I can read it again

My Book Log

Date Read____________

Book Title ____

Author____

I give this book ________ stars ★ ★ ★ ★ ★

What I enjoyed about the book

____
____
____
____
____
____
____
____

What I didn't enjoy about this book

____
____
____
____
____
____
____

What I will do with this book now?

- Donate
- Gift it
- Save it so I can read it again

Date Read____________

Book Title ____

Author____

I give this book _________ stars ★ ★ ★ ★ ★

What I enjoyed about the book

____
____
____
____
____
____
____
____

What I didn't enjoy about this book

____
____
____
____
____
____
____
____

What I will do with this book now?

- ○ Donate
- ○ Gift it
- ○ Save it so I can read it again

Date Read_______________

Book Title ____

Author____

I give this book _________ stars ★ ★ ★ ★ ★

What I enjoyed about the book

____

____

____

____

____

____

____

What I didn't enjoy about this book

____

____

____

____

____

____

____

What I will do with this book now?

- o Donate
- o Gift it
- o Save it so I can read it again

My Book Log

Date Read_____________

Book Title ____

Author____

I give this book _________ stars ★ ★ ★ ★ ★

What I enjoyed about the book

____
____
____
____
____
____
____
____

What I didn't enjoy about this book

____
____
____
____
____
____
____
____

What I will do with this book now?

- o Donate
- o Gift it
- o Save it so I can read it again